Some Cities and San

and Resurgam

Hubert Howe Bancroft

Alpha Editions

This edition published in 2023

ISBN : 9789357960069

Design and Setting By
Alpha Editions
www.alphaedis.com
Email - info@alphaedis.com

SOME CITIES AND SAN FRANCISCO

There had been some discussion as to improving and beautifying the city of San Francisco prior to the catastrophe of April 18th. Landscape architects had been consulted, proposals considered, and preliminary plans drawn. Therefore when on that day the city was swept by fire, obviously it was the opportune moment for the requisite changes in the rebuilding. For a brief period enthusiasm waxed warm. It helped to mitigate the blow, this fencing with fate. Let the earth shake, and fires burn, we will have here our city, better and more beautiful than ever—and more valuable—an imperial city of steel it shall be, and thus will we get even with the misfortunes of this day.

Reform in the rebuilding was needed, whatever should be the scale of beauty or utility decided upon. Fifty years ago the elevating influences of tasteful environment were not so highly appreciated as now, and all large cities are fifty years old or more. All large cities, as a rule, had their beginning with narrow, crooked streets and mean houses. In Europe and Asia there are aggregations of humanity whose domiciles have remained unchanged, one might almost say uncleansed, for hundreds or thousands of years, or ever since their mythical beginning, save only for the covering of the debris of dead centuries.

These ancient towns, mostly offspring of feudalism, begun under castle walls and continued after walls and castle had crumbled, as their area enlarged, with some improvement, perhaps, in the suburban parts, still retained this patch of mediaevalism, until obliterated by war, or fire, or later by modern progress. Look at Edinburgh, for example. With all its Scotch thrift and neatness, there yet remains the ill-conditioned and once filthy quarter, beside which rise the old-time ten-story houses built into the hillside, while in the modern part of the city in sharp contrast are broad streets and open squares and fine buildings.

In America the birth of towns is quite different. Here are no plantings of trembling poverty under lordly walls, but bold pioneering, forecasting agriculture and commerce; no Babel building, with "Go to, let us build here a Cleveland or a Cincinnati," but rather, "Here for the present we will abide." If, however, serfdom and mediaevalism were absent in New World town-planting, so also were aestheticism or any appreciation of the beautiful apart from the useful. Old cities require reconstruction to make them what modern taste and intelligence demand; settlements in their incipiency are dominated by their sturdy founders, who usually have other things to think about than beauty and adornment.

In this day of great wealth and wonderful inventions we realize more and more the value of the city to mankind, and the quality of the city as a means of culture. Cities are not merely marts of commerce; they stand for civility; they are civilization itself. No untried naked Adam in Eden might ever pass for a civilized man. The city street is the school of philosophy, of art, of letters; city society is the home of refinement. When the rustic visits the city he puts on his best clothes and his best manners. In their reciprocal relations the city is as men make it, while from the citizen one may determine the quality of the city. The atmosphere of the city is an eternal force. Therefore as we value the refinement of the human mind, the enlargement of the human heart, we shall value the city, and strive so to build, and adorn, and purify, that it may achieve its ultimate endeavor.

Civic betterment has long been in progress among the more civilized communities through the influence of cultured people capable of appreciating the commercial as well as the aesthetical value of art. Vast sums have been spent and great results accomplished, but they are nothing as compared with the work yet to be done—work which will continue through the ages and be finished only with the end of time.

And not only will larger wealth be yet more freely poured out on artistic adornment, but such use of money will be regarded as the best to which it can be applied. For though gold is not beautiful it can make beauty, even that beauty which elevates and ennobles, which purifies the mind and inspires the soul. Progress is rapid in this direction as in many others. A breach of good taste in public works will ere long be adjudged a crime. For already mediaeval mud has ceased to be fashionable, and the picturesque in urban ugliness is picturesque no longer. All the capitals of Europe have had to be made over, Haussmannized, once or several times. Our own national capital we should scarcely be satisfied with as its illustrious founder left it.

It is a hopeful sign amidst some discouraging ones that wealth as a social factor and measure of merit is losing something of its prestige; that it is no longer regarded by the average citizen as the supreme good, or the pursuit of it the supreme aim in life; there are so many things worth more than money, so many human aspirations and acquirements worthy of higher considerations than the inordinate cravings of graft and greed. Hoarded wealth especially is not so worshipful to-day as it was yesterday, while the beautiful still grows in grace—the beautiful and the useful, compelling improvement, always engendered by improved environment.

Some cities are born in the purple—rare exceptions to the rule. San Francisco is not one of these. St. Petersburg, the city of palaces, of broad avenues and granite-faced quays, whose greatest afflictions are the occasional overflow of the Neva and the dynamite habit, was spoken into being by a monarch. Necessity stands sponsor for Venice, the beautiful, with her streets of water-ways and airs of heavenly harmony; while nature herself may claim motherhood of Swedish Stockholm, brilliant with intermingling lakes islands and canals, rocks hills and forests, rendering escape from the picturesque impossible.

Penn planted his Quakers about 1682, long before many of the present large cities in America were begun, yet Philadelphia was one of the few sketched in such generous proportions that little change was afterwards necessary to make it one of the most spacious of urban commonwealths. With this example before him came in 1791, more than a century later, the father of his country, who permitted his surveyors so injudiciously to cover the spot on the Potomac which he had chosen for the capital city of the republic as to require much expensive remodeling later. Yet what American can drive about Washington now and say it is not worth the cost? Further, as an example, the repeated reconstruction and adornment of the national capital by Congress are priceless to the whole United States, the government therein bearing witness to the value of the beautiful. And if of value on the Potomac, is it not equally so at the portal of the Pacific?

A few other cities there have been which have arisen at the command of man, potentate or pirate, besides those of the quaker Penn and the tzar Peter—Alexandria, the old and the new, with Constantinople between; the first by order of the poor world conqueror, at the hand of the architect Dinocrates, two or three centuries before Caesar, Cleopatra, and Antony, but made fit for them and their chariots by streets a hundred feet wide.

The Danube is the mother of many cities, directing the destiny of nations, from the Iron Gate to the Golden Horn. Vienna has been made brilliantly modern since 1858. Beside the sufferings of Constantinople our little calamity seems tame. Seven times during the last half century the city has been swept by fire, not to mention earthquakes, or pestilence, which on one occasion took with it three hundred thousand lives. Yet all the while it grows in magnificence faster than the invisible enemies of Mohammed can destroy it. But for these purifying fires the city would still be one of narrow, filthy streets and vile smells, reeking with malaria. The Golden Horn of the Bosporus possesses no greater natural advantages than the Golden Gate of San Francisco, nor even so great. The industrial potentialities of the former are not to be compared with those of the latter, while for healthful airs and charming environment we have all that earth can give, and therewith should be content.

Cities have been made as the marquis of Bute made Cardiff, by constructing a dock, and ship canal, and converting the ancient castle into a modern palace. Many towns have been started as railway stations, but few of them attained importance. Steamboat landings have been more fortunate. Some cities owe their origin to war, some to commerce, and not a few to manufactures. Fanaticism has played a part, as in India and parts of Africa, where are nestings of half-savage humanity with a touch of the heavenly in the air. Less disciplined are these than zion—towns, but nearer the happiness of insensibility—the white—marbled and jeweled Taj Mahal, Agra on the Jumna, and Delhi, making immortal Jehan the builder, with his pearl mosque and palace housing the thirty-million-dollar peacock throne; Benares, on the Ganges, a series of terraces and long stone steps extending upward from the holy water, while rising yet higher in the background are temples, towers, mosques, and palaces, all in oriental splendor. Algiers, likewise, an amphitheatre in form, might give San Francisco lessons in terrace construction, having hillsides covered with them, the scene made yet more striking by the dazzling white of the houses. After the place became French, the streets were widened and arcades established in the lower part.

In fact, the French believe in the utility of beauty, and in Paris at least they make it pay. The entire expenses of the municipal government, including police and public works, are met by the spendings of visitors. To their dissolute monarchs were due such creations as the Tuileries, the Louvre, and Versailles. Have we not dissolute millionaires enough to give us at least one fine city?

London and Paris stand out in bold contrast, the one for utility, the other for beauty. Both are adepts in their respective arts. The city proper of London has better buildings and cleaner streets than when St. Paul was erected; otherwise it is much the same. Elsewhere in London, however, are spacious parks and imposing palaces, with now and then a fine bit of something to look out upon, as the bridges of the murky Thames, the Parliament houses, the Abbey, Somerset house, and Piccadilly, perhaps. Children may play at the Zoo, while grown-ups sit in hired chairs under the trees.

Three times London was destroyed by the plague, and five times by fire, that of 1666 lasting four days, and covering thrice the area of the San Francisco conflagration; yet it was rebuilt better than before in three and a half years. Always the city is improved in the rebuilding; how much, depends upon the intelligence and enterprise of the people.

Paris is brilliant with everything that takes the eye—palaces, arches, Bon Marche shops, arcades, colonnades, great open spaces adorned with statues, forest parks, elysian driveways, and broad boulevards cut through mediaeval quarters in every direction, as well for air as for protection from the canaille blockaded in the narrow streets. San Francisco may have some canaille of her own to boast of one of these days; canaille engendered from the scum of Europe and Asia, and educated at our expense for our destruction. Over and over, these two cities, each a world metropolis, have been renovated and reconstructed, the work in fact going on continuously.

For some of the most effective of our urban elaborations we must go back to the first of city builders of whom we have knowledge. The Assyrians made terraces, nature teaching them. On the level plain building ground was raised forty feet for effect. Like all artists of precivilization, the Assyrians placed adornment before convenience, as appeared in Nineveh on the Tigris and Babylon on the Euphrates. At Thebes and Palmyra it was the same, their palaces of alabaster, if one chooses to believe what is said, covering, some of them, a hundred acres. The fashion now is to build upward rather than outward. Besides this alabaster acreage there are to be taken into account the pyramids, artificial mountains, and endless towertowns, supposed to be an improvement on whatever existed before their time. Around the Mediterranean and over India way were once hundreds of charming places like the Megara suburb of Carthage and the amphitheatre of Rhodes, prolific in classic art and architecture, precious gifts of the gods.

But before all other gods or gifts comes Athens, where the men were as gods and the gods very like the men. Encircling the Acropolis hill—most ancient cities had their central hill—the city owes its grandeur to the many temples dedicated to the Olympian deities by the men who made them, made both deities and temples, that long line of philosophers the sublimity of whose thoughts civilization fed on and found expression in the genius of now and then a Pericles or a Phidias.

Twenty times Rome suffered, each time worse than ever befell an American city, the debris of destruction overspreading her sacred soil some fathoms deep, yet all the while mistress of the world.

The Moors in Spain reconstructed and embellished many cities, and built many entire. To them Spain owes her finest specimens of art and architecture, as Seville, Cordova, and the Alhambra. In Naples the mediaeval still overshadows the modern. The city needs cleansing, though she flourishes in her filth and volcanic belchings. Nice, like Paris, plans to please her guests. Berlin was a little late with her reconstructive work; the town walls were not removed till 1866. Though dating from 1190, Glasgow is practically modern, having been several times renovated by fire. Antwerp, burned in 1871, was quickly rebuilt. The Hague is charming as the city of peace. Munich, on the Isar, is every day drifting into the beautiful, not to say aesthetical.

Pekin is a city sui generis, with its Kin-Ching, or prohibited city, sacred to royalty; its Hwang-Ching, or imperial city, exclusively for court officials;

its Tartar division and Chinese division, all completed according to the grand khan and Confucius. Happy Celestials! There is nothing more to be done, nothing to reconstruct, nothing to improve; it stands alone, the only city in all the world that is absolutely finished and perfect. But of a truth our public works sink into insignificance beside those of the ancient barbarians, the great wall and canal of China, the pyramids of Egypt, and the brilliant cities of Assyria and Palmyra.

The cities of Australia—Melbourne, Sydney, Adelaide—in common with all those of the British colonies, are laid out along liberal lines, with broad streets, parks, public squares, and beautiful modern buildings, requiring little change for many years to come. The English part of Calcutta is a city of palaces, built from the spoils of subjugation. Yokohama was a small fishing station when Commodore Perry called there in 1854.

In the New World as in the Old, from John Cotton to Joseph Smith, religion with cupidity inspires. One William Blaxton in 1630 lived where Boston now is, and invited thither Winthrop and his colonists. When banished from Massachusetts, Roger Williams stepped ashore on the bank of the Seekonk, on a rock where is now Providence. The French built a fort where Marquette camped in 1673, and there is now Chicago. Buffalo was a military post in 1812. St. Paul was an Indian trading station prior to 1838. The building of Fort Washington was followed by settlers and Cincinnati was begun. Henry Hudson touched at Manhattan island in 1609, and the Dutch following, New York was the result. Brigham Young, journeying westward, came to the Great Salt Lake, where, as he told his followers, he was instructed by divine revelation to plant the City of the Saints. It proved more permanent than might have been expected, as zion—cities usually are quite ephemeral affairs.

Boston, the beneficial, swept by fires, smallpox, witchcraft, quakerism, snowstorms, earthquakes, and proslavery riots, still lives to meditate upon her own superiority and to instruct mankind. Much attention has been given of late in Boston and suburban towns to artistic effect in street architecture. Until recently New York has given but little thought to pleasing effects. Broadway was not broad, and Fifth Avenue was not striking. Of late, however, the city has become imperial, houses parks and driveways being among the finest in the world. New Orleans has survived at least a dozen great yellow-fever crises since 1812, population meanwhile increasing twentyfold. After the enforced construction of the levee, the idea came to some one that the top of it would make a fine driveway, which in due time was extended from the river and bayous to the lake, thus becoming the most attractive feature of the place. Though not without natural attractions, Chicago was not made by or for her things of beauty. Beginning with low wooden houses along dirty streets, transformations were continued until systems of parks and boulevards with elegant edifices came into view,—which shows that, however material the beginning of American towns may be, if prosperity comes the aesthetical is sure to come with it. A contrast to Chicago may be found in St. Louis, for a long time trading-post town and city, which would be of more importance now were her people of a different quality. Even her chronic calamities, tornadoes, floods, and epidemics, fail to rouse her energies, so that Chicago, starting later and under more adverse circumstances, outstripped her in every particular. Cleveland was laid out for a fine city, so that as she grew little alteration was found necessary. The streets are wide, 80 to 120 feet— Superior Street 132 feet—and so abundant is the foliage, largely maple, that it is called the Forest city.

As an instance of modern aesthetic town construction one might cite Denver, a western Yankee metropolis of ultrarefined men and women from down Boston way, breathing a nomenclature never so freely used before among mid-continent mountains, streets, schoolhouses, parks, and gardens—all alive with the names of New England poets, philosophers, and statesmen. Scarcely yet turned the half century in age, few such charming cities as Denver have been made with fewer mistakes.

San Francisco at her birth and christening had for godfather neither prince nor priest, nor any cultured coterie. The sandy peninsula, on whose inner edge, at the cove called Yerba Buena, stood some hide and tallow stores and fur depots which drew to them the stragglers that passed that way, was about as ill-omened a spot as the one designated by the snake-devouring eagle perched upon an island cactus as the place where the wandering Aztecs should rest and build their city of Mexico. San Francisco's godparents were but common humanity, traders and adventurers, later gold-seekers and pot politicians, intelligent, bold, and for the most part honest; few intending long to remain, few dreaming of the great city to arise here; few caring how the town should be made, if one were made at all. When was improvised an alcalde after the Mexican fashion, and two boards of aldermen were established after the New York fashion, and the high officials saw that they could now and then pick up a twenty-five-dollar fee for deeding a fifty vara lot, if so be they had on hand some fifty varas, they forthwith went to work to make them by drawing lines in front of the cove and intersecting them at right angles by lines running up over the hills, giving their own names, with a sprinkling of the names of bear-flag heroes, not forgetting the usual Washington and Jackson, leaving in the centre a plaza, the cove in front to be filled in later. The streets were narrow, dusty in summer and miry in winter. Spanish-American streets are usually thirty-six feet wide. Winding trails led from the Presidio to the Mission, and from Mission and Presidio to the cove. This was the beginning of San Francisco, which a merciful providence has five times burned, the original shacks and their successors, the last time thoroughly, giving the inhabitants the opportunity to build something better.

All this time the matchless bay and inviting shores awaited the coming of those who should aid in the accomplishment of their high destiny. Situated on the Pacific relatively as is New York on the Atlantic, the natural gateway with its unique portal between the old East and the new West, the only outlet for the drainage of thousands of square miles of garden lands and grain fields, a harbor in the world's center of highest development, with no other to speak of within five hundred miles on either side; dominator of the greatest of oceans, waters more spacious than those of Rio, airs of purple haze sweeter than those of Italy, hills islands and shore lines more sublime than any of Greece—all this time these benefactions of nature have awaited the appreciation and action of those who for their own benefit and the benefit of the nation would utilize them. Are they here now, these new city-builders, or must San Francisco wait for another generation?

They must be men of broad minds, for this is no ordinary problem to be worked out. It is certain that in the near or distant future there will be here a very large and very wealthy city, probably the largest and wealthiest in the world. The whole of the peninsula will be covered, and as much more space beyond it, and around the bay shores to and beyond Carquinez strait. Viewed in the light of history and progressional phenomena, this is the only rational conclusion.

Always the march of intellectual development has been from east to west, the old East dying as the new West bursts into being, until now west is east, and the final issue must here be met. In the advent and progress of civilization there was first the Mediterranean, then the Atlantic, and then the Pacific, the last the greatest of all. What else is possible? Where else on this planet is man to go for his ultimate achievement?

Conviction comes slowly in such cases, and properly so. Yet in forecasting the future from the light of the past cavilers can scarcely go farther afield than our worshipful forbears, who less than a century ago, on the floor of the United States congress, decried as absurd settlement beyond the Missouri, ridiculed buying half a continent of worthless Northwest wilderness, thanked God for the Rocky mountain barrier to man's presumption, scouted at a possible wagon road, not to say railway, across the continent, lamented the unprofitable theft of California, and cursed the Alaska purchase as money worse than thrown away. In view of what has been and is, can anyone call it a Utopian dream to picture the

Pacific bordered by an advanced civilization with cities more brilliant than any of the ancient East, more opulent than any of the cultured West?

Rio de Janeiro! what have the Brazilians been doing these last decades? Decapitating politically dear Dom Pedro, true patriot, though emperor—he came to me once in my library, pouring out his soul for his beloved Brazil—they abolished slavery, formed a republic, and modernized the city. They made boulevards and water drives, the finest in the world. They cut through the heart of the old town a new Avenida Central, over a mile in length and one hundred and ten feet wide, lining it on either side with palatial business houses and costly residences, paving the thoroughfare with asphalt and adorning it with artistic fixtures for illumination, the street work being completed in eighteen months. Strangling in their incipiency graft and greed, after kindly dismissing Dom Pedro with well-filled pockets for home, these Portuguese brought out their money and spent hundreds of millions in improving their city, with hundreds of millions left which they have yet to spend. Thus did these of the Latin race, whom we regard as less Bostonian than ourselves.

With this brief glance at other cities of present and other times, and having in view the part played by environment in the trend of refining influences, and remembering further, following the spirit of the times, that nothing within the scope of human power to accomplish is too vast, or too valuable, or too advanced for the purpose, it remains with the people of San Francisco to determine what they will do.

It is not necessary to speak of the city's present or future requirements, as sea water on the bills, and fresh water with electric power from the Sierra; sea wall, docks, and water-way drives; widened streets and winding boulevards; embellished hillsides and hilltops; bay tunnels and union railway station; bay and ocean boating and bathing; arches and arcades; park strips or boulevards cutting through slums, and the nests of filthy foreigners, bordered on either side by structures characteristic of their country—all this and more will come to those who shall have the matter in charge. The pressing need now is a general plan for all to work to; this, and taking the reconstruction of the city out of politics and placing it in the hands of responsible business men.

If the people and government of the United States will consider for a moment the importance to the nation of a well-fortified and imposing city and seaport at San Francisco bay; the importance to the army and navy, to art and science, to commerce and manufactures; of the effect of a city with its broad surroundings, at once elegant and impressive, upon the nations round the Pacific and on all the world, there should be little trouble in its accomplishment.

And be it remembered that whatever San Francisco, her citizens and her lovers, do now or neglect to do in this present regeneration will be felt for good or ill to remotest ages. Let us build and rebuild accordingly, bearing in mind that the new San Francisco is to stand forever before the world as the measure of the civic taste and intelligence of her people.

RESURGAM

The question has been oftener asked than answered, why Chicago should have grown in wealth and population so much faster than St. Louis, or New Orleans, or San Francisco. It is not enough to point to her position on the lakes, the wide extent of contributory industries, and the convergence of railways; other cities have at their command as great natural advantages with like limitless opportunity. As to location, city sites are seldom chosen by convention, or the fittest spots favored. Chicagoans assert that a worse place than theirs for a city cannot be found on the shores of Lake Michigan. New York would be better up the Hudson, London in Bristol channel, and San Francisco at Carquinez strait. Indeed, it was by a Yankee trick that the sand-blown peninsula secured the principal city of the Pacific.

It happened in this way. General Vallejo, Mexican comandante residing at Sonoma, upon the arrival of the new American authorities said to them: "Let it bear the name of my wife, Francesca, and let it be the commercial and political metropolis of your Pacific possessions, and I will give you the finest site in the world for a city, with state-house and residences built and ready for your free occupation." And so it was agreed, and the general made ready for the coming of the legislature.

Meanwhile, to the American alcalde, who had established his rule at Yerba Buena, a trading hamlet in the cove opposite the island of that name and nucleus of the present San Francisco, came Folsom, United States army captain and quartermaster, to whom had been given certain lots of land in Yerba Buena, and said: "Why not call the town San Francisco, and bring hither ships which clear from various ports for San Francisco bay?" And so it was done; the fine plans of the Mexican general fell to the ground, and the name Benicia was given to what had been Francesca. A year or two later, with five hundred ships of the gold-seekers anchored off the cove, not all the men and money in the country could have moved the town from its ill-chosen location.

Opportunity is much the same in various times and places, whether fortuitous or forced. More men make opportunity than are made by it, particularly among those who achieve great success. Land being unavailable, Venice the beautiful was built upon the water, while the Hollanders manage to live along the centuries below sea level.

The builders of Chicago possessed varied abilities of a high order, not least among which was the faculty of working together. They realized at an early date that the citizens and the city are one; whatever of advantage they might secure to their city would be returned to them by their city fourfold.

"Oh, I do love this old town!" one of them was heard to exclaim as, returning from the station, his cab paddled through the slushy streets under a slushy sky. He was quite a young man, yet he had made a large fortune there. "It's no credit to us making money here," he added, "we couldn't help it." So citizenized, what should we expect if not unity of effort, a willingness to efface self when necessary, and with intense individualism to subordinate individual ideas and feelings to the public good? In such an atmosphere rises quickly a new city from the ashes of the old, or a fairy creation like the Columbian Exposition. Imagine the peninsula of San Francisco covered by a real city equal in beauty and grandeur to the Chicago sham city of 1893.

The typical West-American city builder has money—created, not inherited, wealth. But possession merely is not enough; he gives. Yet possessing and giving are not enough; he works, constantly and intelligently. The power which wealth gives is often employed in retarding progress when the interests of the individual seem to clash with those of the commonwealth; it is always lessened by the absence of respect for its possessor. But when wealth, intelligence, honesty, and enthusiasm join hands with patriotism there must be progress.

Time and place do not account for all of Chicago's phenomenal growth, nor do the distance from the world's centres of population and industry, the comparative isolation, and the evil effects of railway domination account wholly for San Francisco's slow growth toward the end of the century. For, following the several spasms of development incident to the ages of gold, of grain, and of fruit, and the advent of the railway incubus, California for a time betook herself to rest, which indeed was largely paralysis. Then, too, those who had come first and cleared the ground, laying the foundations of fortunes, were passing away, and their successors seemed more ready to enjoy than to create. But with the opening of a new century all California awoke and made such progress as was never made before.

Coming to the late catastrophe, it was well that too much dependence was not placed on promises regarding rehabilitation made during the first flush of sympathy; the words were nevertheless pleasant to the ear at the time. The insurance companies would act promptly and liberally, taking no advantage of any technicality; congress would remit duties on building material for a time, and thus protect the city-builders from the extortions of the material men; the material men roundly asserted that there should be no extortion, no advance in prices, but, on the contrary, all other work should be set aside and precedence given to San Francisco orders; eastern capitalists were to cooperate with the government in placing at the portal of the Pacific a city which should be a credit to the nation and a power in the exploitation of the great ocean.

None of these things came to pass. Indeed it was too much to expect of poor human nature until selfishness and greed are yet further eliminated. Never to be forgotten was the superb benevolence which so promptly and so liberally showered comforts upon the poor, the sick, the hungry, and the houseless until it was feared that the people might become pauperized. But that was charity, whereas "business is business."

The insurance companies, themselves stricken nigh unto death, paused in the generous impulse to pay quickly and in full and let the new steel city arise at once in all its glory. They began to consider, then to temporize, and finally, with notable exceptions, to evade by every means in their power the payment of their obligations. The loss and the annoyance thus inflicted upon the insured were increased by the uncertainty as to what they should finally be able to do. Congress likewise paused to consider the effect the proposed remission of duties would have on certain members and their lumber and steel friends. Thus a hundred days passed by, and with some relief half a hundred more.

Outside capital was still ready, but San Franciscans seemed to have sufficient for present needs. Capital is conservative and Californians independent. Even from the government they never asked much, though well aware that since the gold discovery California has given a hundredfold more than she has received. Her people were accustomed to take care of themselves, and managed on the whole to get along. A general conflagration was not a new thing. Four times during gold-digging days San Francisco was destroyed by fire, and each time new houses were going up before the ashes were cold. True, there was not so much to burn in those days, but it was all the people had; there was not so much to rebuild, and there were no insurance companies to keep them back. San Francisco would be grateful, and it would be a graceful thing for the government to do, to keep away the sharks until the people should get their heads above water again, not as charity, but for the general good. The exaction of duties on lumber from British Columbia was simply taking money from the San Francisco builders and thrusting it into the plethoric pockets of the Puget Sound people, who at once advanced their prices so as seriously to retard building and render it in many cases impossible. Even as I write word comes of another advance in the price of lumber, owing to the apathy at Washington and elsewhere, after twice before raising the price to the highest limit.

Meanwhile, in and around the burned district, traffic never ceased. The inflow of merchandise from all parts continued. Upon the ashes of their former stores, and scattered about the suburbs, business men established themselves wherever they could find a house to rent or a lot to build upon. Shacks were set up in every quarter, and better structures of one or two stories were permitted, subject to removal by order of the city at any time they should appear to stand in the way of permanent improvement. Some business houses were extinguished, but other and larger ones arose in their stead. Rebuilding was slow because of the debris to be removed and the more substantial character of the permanent structures to be erected.

Around the bay continues the hum of industry. The country teems with prosperity. Never were the services of the city needed so much as now. There are no financial disturbances; money is easy, but more will be required soon; claims are not pressed in the courts. Any San Francisco bonds thrown upon the market are quickly taken by local capitalists. Customs receipts are larger than ever before, and there is no shrinkage at the clearing house. Land values remain much the same; in some quarters land has depreciated, in other places it has increased in price; buyers stand ready to take advantage of forced sales.

Labor is scarce in both city and country; wages are high and advancing. Five times the present number of mechanics can find profitable employment in the city, and it will be so for years to come, as there is much to be done.

With the advance of the labor wage and of lumber, rents are advanced. Mills and factories are running at their full capacity. Orchards and grain fields are overflowing, and harvesters are found with difficulty. Merchants' sales were never so large nor profits so good. Prices of everything rule high, with an upward tendency, the demand at the shops being for articles of good quality. Oriental rugs and diamonds are conspicuously in evidence. Insurers are paying their losses to some extent, and many people find themselves in possession of more ready money than they ever had before. They are rich, though they may have no house to sleep in. It is a momentary return to the flush times of the early fifties, though upon a broader and more civilized scale, and without their uncertainty or their romance.

In view of the facts it seems superfluous to discuss questions regarding the future of San Francisco. That is to say, such questions as are propounded by chronic croakers: Will the city be rebuilt? If so, will it be a city of fine buildings? Will not the fear of earthquakes drive away capital and confine reconstruction to insignificance?

Let us hasten to assure our friends that the day of doom has not yet come to this city; that the day of doom never comes to any city for so slight a cause, or for any cause short of a rain of brimstone and fire, as in the case of Sodom. Whether of imperial steel or of imperial shacks; whether calamities come in the form of such temblores as are here met occasionally in a mild form, or in the far more destructive form of hurricanes, floods, pestilence, sun—striking, and lightning, so common at the east and elsewhere, and from which San Francisco is wholly free, there will here forever be a city, a large, powerful, and wealthy city.

Every part of the earth is subject at any time to seismic disturbance, and no one can truthfully say that California is more liable to another such occurrence than any other part of the United States. Indeed, it should be less so, the earth's crust here having settled itself, let us hope, to some centuries of repose. Never before has anything like this been known on our Pacific seaboard. Never before, so far as history or tradition or the physical features of the country can show, has California experienced a serious earthquake shock—that is to say, one attended by any considerable loss of life or property. Nor was the earthquake of April last so terrible as it may seem to some. Apart from the fire there was not so very much of it, and no great damage was done. The official figures are: 266 killed by falling walls, 177 by fire, 7 shot, and 2 deaths by ptomaine poisoning—452 in all. The property damage by the earthquake is scarcely worth speaking of, being no more than happens elsewhere in the world from other causes nearly every day; it would have been quickly made good and little thought of it but for the conflagration that followed.

Compare San Francisco casualties with those of other cities. Two hundred and sixty-six deaths as the result of the greatest calamity that ever happened in California! Not to mention the floods, fires, and cyclones common to St. Louis, Chicago, Galveston, and all mid-continent America, the yellow fever at New Orleans and along the southern shore, or the 25,000 deaths from cholera in New York and Philadelphia in less than twenty-five years, or the loss of 1,000 ships on the Atlantic coast in the hurricane of August, 1873-not to mention the many extraordinary displays of vindictive nature, take some of the more commonplace calamities incident to most cities except those along the Pacific coast.

Every year more people and more property are destroyed by lightning, floods, and wind-storms on the Atlantic side of the Rocky mountains than are affected by earthquakes on the Pacific side in a hundred years. Every year more people drop dead from sunstrokes in New York, Baltimore, Philadelphia, and other eastern cities than are killed by earthquakes in San Francisco in a thousand years, so far as we may know. Yet men and women continue to live and build houses in those cities without thought of running away.

Nor can California claim the whole even of United States earthquakes. In 1755 all New England was shaken up, and Boston housetops and walls were set dancing, the horror coming in "with a roaring noise, like that of thunder," as the record has it, "and then a swell like the roaring sea"; and yet, and notwithstanding the great fire later, the city still shows vitality, the people are not afraid, and property is valuable. And so in regard to New York and London and all cities. In Missouri, in 1811, the earth shook almost continuously for several months along a stretch of three hundred miles, throwing up prairies into sand hills and submerging forests. Chicago and New York, and all the country between, were visited by earthquakes in 1870. Then there are Virginia and the Carolinas, Alabama Texas and Colorado—there is not a state in the union that has not had a touch of well-authenticated earthquakings at some time in its history.

To one who knows the people and the country, the people with their magnificent energy and ability, their indomitable will and their splendid courage; the country with its boundless natural wealth and illimitable potentialities; the city, key to the Golden Gate, which opens the East to the West and West to East; the bay, mistress primeval, through which flows the drainage of six hundred miles in length of interior valley, the garden of the world; to one who has here lived and loved, assisting in this grand upbuilding, thoughts of relinquishment, of lesser possibilities, of meaner efforts, do not come.

What would you? If there is a spot on earth where life and property are safer, where men are more enterprising and women more intelligent and refined, where business is better or fortunes more safely or surely made, the world should know of it. The earth may tremble now and then, but houses may be built which cannot be destroyed, fires are liable to occur wherever material exists that will burn, but fires may be controlled.

As for the city, its life and destiny, there is this to be said. The few square miles of buildings burned were not San Francisco, they were only buildings. Were every house destroyed and every street obliterated, there would still remain the city, with its commerce, its manufactures, its civilization, a spiritual city if you like, yet with material values incapable of destruction— an atmosphere alive with cheerful industry; also land values, commercial relations, financial connections, skilled laborers and professional men, and a hundred other like souls of things. In a thousand ideas and industries, though the ground is but ashes, the spirit of progress still hovers over the hills awaiting incarnation. Dependent on this pile of ashes, or the ghosts thereof, are fleets of vessels sailing every sea; farms and factories along shore and back to and beyond the Sierra; merchants and mechanics here and elsewhere; mines and reclamation systems, and financial relations the world over.

The question now is not as to the existence or permanency of a central city on the shores of San Francisco bay. That fact was established beyond peradventure with the building of the bay, and nothing short of universal cataclysm can affect it. It is rather to the quality of that city that the consideration of the present generation should be directed. The shell has been injured, but the soul of the city is immortal; and in the restoration it would be strange if our twentieth-century young men cannot do better in artistic city building than the sturdy gold-seekers and their successors of half a century ago.

If history and human experiences teach anything; if from the past we may judge somewhat of the future, we might, if we chose, glance back at the history of cities, and note how, when the Mediterranean was the greatest of seas, Carthage and Venice were the greatest of cities; how, when the Atlantic assumed sway, Ghent, Seville, and London each in turn came to the front; or how, following the inevitable, as civilization takes possession of the Pacific, the last, the largest in its native wealth as well as in its potentialities the richest of all, it is not difficult to see that the chief city, the mistress of this great ocean, must be mistress of the world.

But this is not all. A great city on this great bay, beside this greatest of oceans, centrally situated, through whose Golden Gate pass the waters drained from broad fertile valleys, a harbor without an equal, with some hundreds of miles of water front ready for a thousand industries, where ocean vessels may moor beside factories and warehouses, with a climate temperate, equable, healthful, and brewed for industry; a city here, ugly or beautiful, fostered or oppressed, given over to the sharks of speculation or safeguarded as one of the brightest jewels of the nation, is an inexorable necessity; its destiny is assured; and all the powers of graft and greed cannot prevail against it. It is a military necessity, for here will be stationed the chief defenses and defenders of the nation's western border. It is an industrial necessity, for to this city three continents and a thousand islands will look for service. As the Spanish war first revealed to America her greatness, so the possible loss of San Francisco quickly demonstrates the necessity of her existence to the nation. It is an educational necessity, whence the dusky peoples around the Pacific may draw from the higher civilization to the regeneration of the world. In the University of California, standing opposite the Golden Gate, with its able and devoted president and professors, this work is already well established, the results from which will prove too vast and far-reaching for our minds at present to fathom.

And in all the other many byways of progress the results of the last half-century of effort on our sand-dune peninsula are not lost. Earthquakes cannot destroy them; fire cannot burn them. San Francisco grew from the Yerba Buena hamlet in sixty years. In a new and untried field city-building then was something of an experiment; yet population grew to half a million, and wealth in proportion; and never was improvement so marked as just before the fire. With wealth and population but little impaired, and with the ground cleared for new constructive work, there would be nothing strange in a city here of three or four millions of people in another sixty years. Actual progress has scarcely been arrested. We are rudely hustled and awake to higher and severer effort. No house or store or factory or business will be rebuilt or established except in a larger and more efficient way, and that is progress.

In and around the city are already more people than were here before the fire, and soon there will be twice as many, for from every quarter are coming mechanics and business men, attracted by high wages and the material requirements of the city. Hundreds of millions of money from the insurance companies and from local and outside capitalists are finding safe and profitable investment. And this is only the beginning.

San Francisco is already a large manufacturing city; it will be many times larger. Around its several hundred miles of bay shore and up the Carquinez strait will be thousands of industries to-day not dreamed of, and all ministering to the necessities of the thousand cities of the Pacific. There is no place in the world better adapted for manufacturing. All sorts of raw material can be gathered here from every quarter of the earth at small cost, lumber, coal, iron, wool, and cotton for a hundred factories, and mineral ores for reduction. Likewise labor at a minimum wage, congress and the lords of labor permitting. Add to these advantages a climate cool in summer and warm in winter, where work can be comfortably carried on every day in the year, and a more desirable spot cannot be found.

Industrially San Francisco should dominate the Pacific, its firm land and islands, upon whose borders is to be found more natural wealth, mineral and agricultural, than upon those of all the other waters of the earth combined, and the exploitation of which has scarcely begun. Here in abundance are every mineral and metal, rich and varied soils, all fruits and native products, fuels and forests, for some of which we may even thank earthquakes and kindred volcanic forces. Manufactures compel commerce, and the commerce of the Pacific will rule the world. The essentials of commerce are here. Intelligence and enterprise are here and open to enlargement.

For the late severe loss the city may find some compensations—as the cleansing effect of fire; much filth, material and moral, has been destroyed. Yet one is forced to observe that the precincts of Satan retain their land values equal to any other locality. The greatest blessing of the destruction, however, is in the saving from a life of luxury and idleness our best young men and women, who will in consequence enter spheres of usefulness, elevating and ennobling, thus exercising a beneficial influence on future generations. Already work has become the fashion; snobbism is in disgrace; and some elements or influences of the simple life thus reestablished will remain.

When all has been said that may be regarding the present and the future, regarding purposes and potentialities, the simple fact remains that the city of San Francisco will be what people make of it, neither more nor less. The fruitful interior and the pine-clad Sierra; the great ocean, its islands and opulent shores, with their fifty thousand miles of littoral frontage, and every nation thereon awaiting a higher culture than any which has yet appeared; the Panama canal, the world's highway, linking east and west, all these will be everything or nothing to those who sit at the Golden Gate, according as they themselves shall determine. For the glory of a city is not altogether in its marble palaces and structures of steel, though these have their value, but in its citizens, its men and women, its men of ability, of unity, of energy, and public spirit, and its brave and true women. And has not this city these? Surely, if in the late catastrophe all that is noble, benevolent, and self-effacing did not appear in every movement of our people, then no such qualities exist anywhere. The manner in which they rose to meet the emergency argues well for the city's future. Before the calamity was fairly upon them they sprang to grapple it and ward it off so far as possible. It was owing to them and to the military that the city was saved from starvation, anarchy, and disease. It also speaks well for men so severely stricken to be the first to send aid to a similarly stricken city, the metropolis of Pacific South America.

All this leads us to the highest hopes for the future. What we need most of all is a centralization of mechanical industries around the shores of this bay. Let everything that is made be made here, and the requirements of all the peoples facing this ocean here be met. The Panama canal will be a blessing or a curse to California in proportion as she rises to the occasion and makes opportunities. Manufactures and commerce tell the whole story. Let us have the city beautiful by all means—it will pay; Paris makes it pay; but we must have the useful in any event—this, and a municipality with its several parts subordinated to a general scheme. What we can do without is demagogism, with its attendant labor wrangles, and all the fraud, lying, and hypocrisy incident to a too free government. We want a city superior to any other in beauty, as well as in utility, and it will pay these United States well to see that we have it. If we build no better than before, we gain nothing by this fire which has cost many a heartache.

The game of the gods is in our hands; shall we play it worthily? Two decades of inaction at this juncture, like those which followed the advent of the overland railway, would decide the fate of the city adversely for the century, and the effect of it would last for ten centuries. When the shores of the Pacific are occupied as the shores of the Atlantic now are, when all around the vast arena formed by America, Asia, and Australia are great nations of wealth and culture, with hundreds of Bostons and Baltimores, of Londons and Liverpools, the great American republic would scarcely be satisfied with only a porter's lodge at her western gateway.

It is not much to say that the new city will be modern and up to date, with some widened streets and winding boulevards, gardens banging to the hillside, parks with lakes and cascades, reservoirs of sea water on every hilltop; public work and public service, street cars telephones and lighting being of the best. Plans for such changes were prepared before the fire; they can be extended and carried out with greater facility since the ground has been cleared from obstructions. All this and more may easily be done if the government can be made to see where the true interests of the people lie, to regard a west-coast metropolis with an eye for something of beauty as well as of utility, an eye which can see utility in beauty, and withal an eye of pride in possession. A paltry two or three hundred millions judiciously expended here by the government would make a city which would ever remain the pride of the whole people and command the admiration and respect of all the nations around this great ocean.

Of what avail are art and architecture if they may not be employed in a cause like this? Here is an opportunity which the world has never before witnessed. With limitless wealth, with genius of as high an order as any that has gone before, with the stored experiences of all ages and nations—what better use can be made of it all than to establish at the nation's western gate a city which shall be the initial point of a new order of development? Away back in the days of Palmyra and Thebes the rulers of those cities seemed to understand it, if the people did not—that is to say, the value of embellishment. And had we now but one American Nebuchadnezzar we might have a Babylon at our Pacific seaport. For a six-months' world's fair any considerable city can get from the government five or ten millions. And why not? There's politics in it.

Can we not have some of "those politics" for a respectable west-coast city? Would it not be economy to spend some millions on an industrial metropolis which should be a permanent world's fair for the enlightenment of the Pacific? The nation has made its capital beautiful, and so established the doctrine that art, architecture, and beautiful environment have a value above ugly utility. May we not hope for something a little out of the common for the nation's chief seaport on the Pacific, a little fresh gilding for our Golden Gate?

THE END

Milton Keynes UK
Ingram Content Group UK Ltd.
UKHW010706240424
441619UK00004B/292